Sleepy Bedti

A revolutionary

sleep at night

To Lucy

All the best

Dan Jones

Connect With Dan Jones:

www.ALT-Solutions.org/parenting

First Edition 2015

Published By Dan Jones

Copyright © Daniel Jones 2015

Daniel Jones asserts the moral right to be identified as the author of this work

ISBN 978-1517364243

Contents

Introduction   **5**

About This Book   *10*

A Bit About Me & Why I Have Written This Book   *13*

Sleepy Bedtime Tales   **19**

The Rabbit Who Came to Tea   *21*

Timmy and the Secret Door   *28*

The Princess and the Magical Kitten   *35*

The Magical Unicorn   *43*

The Spaceman and the Dinosaur   *50*

The Swift and the Swallow   *58*

The Caterpillar's Dream   *67*

The Boy Who Ran Off to the Circus   *74*

Adventure of a Time-Travelling Worm   *81*

The Puppy Who Wanted to Play   *89*

The Magical Journey Asleep   *98*

Introduction

While I was working in residential children's homes in the early 2000s, I used to be able to get children to sleep where other staff struggled. What I was doing differently to the other staff was applying knowledge I had learnt from studying rapport building and the way in which people respond to each other.

I have had a fascination with how people communicate with each other instinctively since my teens. As a child, I found it difficult to relate to - and understand - others. Luckily, by the age of eight or so, I had started to practise meditation, although it was a few more years before I realised that is what I was doing. To me, I had just found a way of managing anxiety and a way to relax and become focused.

By fourteen, I had discovered hypnosis after seeing Paul McKenna on TV. That transformed my life. I began studying hypnosis; I learnt that the study of hypnosis is the study of the way people communicate unconsciously with each other.

I learnt about an incredible psychiatrist called Dr Milton Erickson, and about his ideas and observations of people. I read all 1,500+ pages of his collected works - a collection of all the papers he wrote throughout his lifetime.

One of these papers stood out for me. The paper was on something he called 'subliminal auditory stimulation'. It was a fascinating paper about how we fall into rapport with each other's breathing patterns. Erickson talked about using his breathing technique to help children sleep by matching and then guiding their breathing from a wakeful to a sleeping breathing pattern.

While working in children's homes, I had the opportunity to see how well the technique worked with a wide range of children of all ages. I found it difficult to create the context to use this approach on older children and teenagers, although the technique does still work if you can find a way of applying it. I found that very young children respond well to the breathing technique just by being present with them, and that children between the ages of about four and seven respond well to the technique when it is done within the context of something else, like reading a bedtime story to them, or watching TV.

I have carried out the technique while reading a story or watching TV to children aged eight to ten years old, but for children in this age range, it does depend on whether reading them a story at night is what they want. I have 'read' my wife to sleep before, so I know it works with any age range up to adulthood - provided the person you are reading to is happy to listen along while you read.

This book isn't about watching TV to help children sleep, so only briefly will I mention what I would do when watching TV with a child as they fall asleep - for it is a slightly different process.

When watching TV with a child I would make sure it is a cartoon or children's programme that they like, it may well be pre-recorded from earlier in the day, or maybe on a DVD. The important thing is that you know it isn't too energetic and that it is something age-appropriate for them to watch. Ideally, it would be something they enjoy watching, but not something that has them wanting to dance or be otherwise active, and certainly not something that makes them laugh too much.

You need to be able to watch it in the child's bedroom where they can be resting in bed, and you can perhaps sit on the edge of their bed, or on a chair next to them. Make sure the room is dark, and the TV isn't too noisy.

While you are both watching the TV, it can help to be stroking the child's arm, back or hair in time with their breathing. After a while, you can begin to slow down the stroking. Their breathing will slow as the stroking does; this helps to guide your child to sleep.

After few minutes of watching the TV, yawn a couple of times over the next minute or so. Then, after yawning, tell your child that you are feeling tired and may miss the end of the programme, so they should make sure they stay awake to let you know what happens.

At this point, the child will usually try to stay awake, but the act of trying to stay awake becomes something that increases the likelihood of them shortly falling asleep. This is how our minds work. Most people who have tried to stay awake to watch a late-night film will have experienced falling asleep before the film starts. Most people will also have experienced wanting to get an early night because you have to be up early in the morning, only to find you can't fall asleep.

The same thing happens with children. You have more chance of getting them to fall asleep if you to tell them to try to stay awake, than if you tell them to try to fall asleep.

Once you have yawned a few times, and then said you are tired and might fall asleep, you can then close your eyes, still matching the breathing of your child, before slowing your breathing down, as a way of guiding them to do the same. Then, keep your eyes closed and relax through to the end of the programme.

Normally, parents joke with me that they have no problem closing their eyes and pretending to fall asleep - rather, the challenge is trying to stay awake while their eyes are closed and they are relaxing!

Once the TV programme ends, you can then open your eyes, gently yawn and stretch, and see if your child is asleep or not. Usually they are, so you can just turn off the TV and quietly leave the room. If they aren't, usually they are so relaxed and tired that you can turn off the TV and say goodnight, saying that you are tired and have to go to sleep now. They will generally accept this and fall asleep.

Sometimes, though, they may still be awake. They are likely to be almost asleep, so you can yawn and sit with them with their eyes closed as you stroke their arm, back or hair, again in time with their breathing. Once more, slow the stroking down so that you guide their breathing to being more relaxed, and also gradually slow down your breathing. After a while, you will notice that they have fallen asleep.

Normally, you will notice a significant shift in their breathing, perhaps changes in how much they are fidgeting, and you may notice twitching. Once you notice these signs that they are asleep, then you can leave their bedroom.

About This Book

This book is aimed at parents of four- to seven-year-olds. There are no pictures in this book, because the children will have their eyes shut as they listen along, allowing them to create the characters in their mind.

It can be good to ask your child to draw the characters from a story and to colour them in, and have a discussion with them about what they may look like. This will make it more personal to your child.

The stories in this book are designed to be read with a slow and calm voice. There are some words in italics; these words are to be read with a brief pause before and after them, and to be read with a bit more relaxing emphasis. For a demonstration of one of the stories being read, visit www.alt-solutions.org/books-3

Each story is about ten minutes long. This is a good length of time to allow your child to fall asleep. If they aren't asleep at the end of a story and you think they are unlikely to go to sleep if you leave the room, then you could always read them another story. If they are asleep but they wake up during the night, you can always read them another story to help them fall asleep again.

These stories work based on a number of psychological principles and techniques. Matching the breathing helps to build rapport with your child, where they can then start to respond to changes that you make within yourself. So if you start to slow down your breathing, this begins to slow down the breathing of your child. Adding emphasis to certain words and phrases associated with relaxing or sleep, and doing this with a slightly more relaxing sleepy tone of voice, primes your child with the idea for sleep - without directly saying sleep to them. Yawning seems to be something that rapidly triggers rapport with others, making others want to yawn in return. This yawning also has the priming effect of triggering the idea of sleep, and is one of the most powerful triggers. It is very difficult to resist a yawn, and even more difficult to resist a yawn when you aren't thinking about trying to resist it. In fact, many people will find that just reading about yawning triggers the desire to yawn.

Top tips for preparing for bedtime:

- Put the house to sleep. A few hours before your child is due to go to bed, start making the house quieter and more relaxed; turn down the lights, draw the curtains, and make everything quiet (like the TV);

- Relaxing time before bed. A few hours before bed, start to focus on relaxation; have children do only relaxing and calm activities. This includes not having emotionally arousing TV or computer games on;

- Get ready for bed early. Have the children get ready into their pyjamas early and start focusing on how long is left before bedtime. Focus on what they want to do before bed;

- Ideally, no tablet PCs, mobile phones, TVs or other electronic devices with a screen, within a couple of hours of bedtime.

Doing all of this improves how bedtime will go. Obviously every family is different, and not all of this will be easy to do in all families, but it helps to do as many of these as possible, or at least to find your own best way to do as close to these as you can.

A Bit About Me & Why I Have Written This Book

I thought I would explain a bit about me, and why I have ended up writing this book.

I have already explained that I developed an interest in meditation and hypnosis while growing up. I explained that I struggled to relate to others, and would sometimes get anxious and need to escape into my mind to find peace.

I have Asperger's Syndrome, a high-functioning form of autism. This means that I can do well intellectually, but I struggle with social situations and struggle to understand others. Luckily for me, I saw Paul McKenna on TV when I was younger, so I developed an obsessive interest in hypnosis and communication skills. As a result of this, I have spent years learning how to do what many others find instinctive; this knowledge has helped me understand how to help guide people into different states of mind, such as relaxation and sleep.

During the early 2000s, I helped to set up a therapeutic home for young children. Prior to this, I had worked in children's homes with teenagers. During my time in the children's home, I used the techniques described here to help the children sleep. There were no books out, as far as I was aware, designed specifically for this technique, so I used to read whatever the child wanted to hear. The story isn't that important; it is the technique which guides the child to sleep (although the technique can be enhanced when using a story designed specifically with these techniques in mind).

At the time I was working in children's homes, parenting programmes were beginning to appear on TV. When it came to tackling sleep, they seemed to all promote similar ideas. They all seemed to advocate that which, in my opinion, caused distress to a child while they were in their bedroom, rather than inducing relaxation for the child.

I saw techniques like holding the child's bedroom door shut while the child cried and screamed on the other side of the door. To me, this is wrong. This kind of technique elicits the wrong emotions in the child and generates the wrong associations with their bedroom and with bedtime.

We are all creatures of association. If something that makes us feel bad happens somewhere, we associate that location with those bad feelings. Likewise, if something good happens somewhere, we associate that location with good feelings.

So, the café in which a loved one broke up with you as a teenager may, for the next few years at least, remind you that this is where you and your partner split up. You will remember exactly which seats you were sitting in, and if you sit in those seats again, the thoughts and feelings of that past experience will be stronger.

The beach where a husband fumbled around awkwardly as he got down on one knee, nervously and romantically proposing to you, becomes a place that brings you pleasant feelings. If you visit the beach you recall that pleasant experience and feel those feelings. And just thinking about going there is likely to begin the process of recalling; the closer to the location you are, the stronger the inner experience is.

The same is true with children. If a child experiences anger and anxiety in their bedroom, then they will begin to associate these feelings with being in their bedroom. This is why it isn't good to use 'go to your room' as a punishment; if the child then experiences being upset, anxious or angry, they may subconsciously associate these feelings with being in their room. This then could impact on their ability to find their room a relaxing and safe place to be, which may prevent them falling asleep so easily at night.

In 2006, I wrote my first parenting book, *Parenting Techniques That Work*, in order to share ideas that I termed "radical" to parenting. I thought of them as being radical, because many of them were so different to other parenting ideas at the time. In the book, I explained how to carry out these various techniques for helping to get children to sleep. I always had the intention of writing a book of stories designed specifically for optimising the various techniques. Some of the elements of these techniques work with any story, whereas other elements can't be done very well with most ordinary stories. One such technique is giving ideas for sleep during the story. This doesn't crop up very often in many books, yet it can make what you do even more effective.

It has taken nearly a decade for me to get round to writing this very book. I have made YouTube videos about the technique; I have made videos telling traditional fairytale stories with these added techniques to help children sleep; I have even made videos using the techniques with Sackboy from the PlayStation3 ™ game Little Big Planet speaking on the video to guide children to sleep. There have always been other books I have had to write first.

What led me to finally write this book was realising that, other than my *Parenting Techniques That Work* book, there is no other book teaching this approach for quickly and calmly getting children to sleep. I felt that - instead of just writing how to do it and expecting parents to use just some of the techniques they can use when reading any book - I would write stories tailored specifically to the techniques, almost like 'guided meditations for children'. I wanted to write the stories so that they wouldn't just help children to sleep, but each story would have a positive message that, with regular use, can begin to help the child with their own personal development as they grow up.

So for me, the reason for writing this book is to share a better way of settling children at night: to give parents stories they can read to their children, designed specifically to help your children fall asleep, rather than resorting to parenting technique that cause anxiety and distress for your child, or resorting to shouting or getting angry with your child for not getting to sleep. Such behaviour only results in further distress for the child, and makes them less likely to sleep.

Sleepy Bedtime Tales

These stories should all take about ten minutes to read. They are written to be read slowly and calmly. Before reading a story to your child, make sure they have been to the toilet and done anything else that they need to do, so that they can fall asleep while following the story; they should have nothing else they need to be doing instead.

When you start the story, make sure your child is in bed and comfortable. Suggest that they close their eyes while you read to them. This will help to ensure that they are able to fall asleep during your reading.

If your child says that they keep falling asleep before the end of the story and they want to know how it ends, then one approach you can take is to tell them that when they fall asleep, they can dream the end of the story and tell you how the story ended in the morning.

As you read the stories, it is good to read in time with when your child breathes out. If they are breathing too fast, you can read in time with two, or even three breaths. Pause briefly as your child breathes in, and then read as they breathe out. If, for example, you are reading across three breaths then you would: read as they breath out, still be reading as they breathe in, then still be reading as they breathe out and in again, and finish the sentence you are reading as they breathe out. Then, pause as they breathe in, before then repeating the same as above for the next cycle of three breaths.

As well as reading in time with their breathing, it is good to yawn a few times during the reading, and have some pauses where you are quiet - perhaps just after you have yawned.

It is best not to overthink all this. There are words highlighted in italics on which you should add emphasis, and as long as you are reading slowly and calmly and doing your best to read in time with your child's breathing, you will be doing well. It can sometimes take practice to get all the elements in place. As you get more of the elements, the process of reading your child to sleep will become more effective and it will begin to feel more natural to read bedtime stories in this way.

The Rabbit Who Came to Tea

As you close your eyes, I'm going to tell you about a rabbit who came to tea. This was no ordinary rabbit; this was Malcolm, the magic rabbit.

So with *your eyes closed*, you can listen to me reading this story, and while I read this story, you can *begin to feel relaxed*. And as I read, you can *imagine this story* and begin to *drift off to sleep*. As *you drift off asleep* you *can continue this story in a dream*. And my reading will help *you feel sleepy*, it will help *you feel tired* and it will help *you fall asleep*.

Malcolm lived inside a magician's hat, and the hat lived on the magician's head. The magician used to spend every day doing magic tricks for children. He would make ribbons appear in his hands, and coins appear from behind the children's ears.

But what the children most loved was when he would show them his magic hat. The magician would show that the hat was empty, and then, with a magic word 'abracadabra' and a wave of his magic wand, there would be a puff of smoke; Malcolm the rabbit would appear out of the hat.

The magician didn't know where Malcolm came from, or where he went when he put him back in the hat. All he knew was that, when he said 'abracadabra' and waved his magic wand, Malcolm would appear in a puff of smoke.

Every evening, the magician went home for his tea. He would take his hat off and leave it on a shelf by the front door until he next went out to do magic for the children. What the magician didn't know was that the hat was magical.

Inside the hat was a magical world. Each day, after the magician's last show, Malcolm travelled *deep down* into the hat and went back home. As he travelled *deeper and deeper* into the hat, he became less aware of the magician's world, and started to become more aware of his own.

His land was one where trees grew upside-down, and the sky was bright pink. When Malcolm arrived home, he found a letter waiting for him on the doormat.

'You are invited to afternoon tea at three. From, Cybil the Squirrel.' Malcolm read.

'Afternoon tea? That does sound nice,' Malcolm thought to himself as he wiped his feet on the doormat and closed the front door behind him.

Malcolm hadn't been to afternoon tea for a long time; he wondered what he should wear. He tried on five different pairs of shoes and four different t-shirts before he decided on the right one for him. He didn't have long to get ready, and he knew *deep down* that he was going to enjoy his afternoon tea.

Once Malcolm was dressed for afternoon tea, he left his house to go and visit his friend, Cybil the Squirrel. Cybil had short ears and a bushy tail, and she lived in the tallest upside-down tree in the land.

Malcolm hopped along the blue path, past the green upside-down oak tree, before turning left. From here, he could see Cybil's tree at the end of the road.

He hopped towards the grand upside-down tree where he found a doorway. He knocked on the door three times.

Knock, knock, knock.

On the third knock, he could hear Cybil's voice. 'Hello, who is it?'

'Hi! It's me, Malcolm'

Just then, the door creaked open and Malcolm could see stairs leading down into the base of the tree. There were ten steps for Malcolm to follow, and each step led Malcolm *deeper and deeper* into the tree. The stairway was lined with twinkling lights, sparkling and flashing with a rainbow of colours, and at the bottom was a beautiful glow coming from a room at the base of the tree.

Malcolm excitedly hopped down the stairs towards the glowing room. The stairs were numbered, to let visitors know how many steps they had left to walk down.

He stepped onto step *ten*, then *nine*, and *eight*. He didn't know what the afternoon tea was going to be like, or what the room at the bottom of the stairs was like. *Seven, six, five*. He was hopping down the stairs *deeper and deeper* into the tree. He began to feel like he was going to a party. *Four, three*. Malcolm was now nearly at the bottom of the stairs and he could see that the room was glowing with a soft light, and he could hear a voice talking in the room. Malcolm continued to hop *deeper and deeper* down into the base of the upside-down tree. *Two, one.*

Malcolm reached the bottom of the tree, paused for a moment, and then stepped into the room.

Cybil was sat in the room at the end of a long table. On the table were lots of plates, full to the brim with small sandwiches, cakes and sweets. Chugging around the outside of the table was a small stream train, pulling carriages laden with tasty food.

Malcolm's mouth watered at the sight of all the food. As he sat down with Cybil to eat, he wondered why she was having this afternoon tea, and why she had invited him round. But, before he could ask, he already had a tasty cake in his mouth. It looked so nice, he couldn't help himself.

'Mm, these are good!' he said, talking with his mouth full.

'Malcolm, I need your help,' Cybil said, 'I have lost my favourite toy. You know magic, and you know how to find things. I need you to help me find my favourite toy.'

Malcolm did know magic, but he didn't know whether he could find Cybil's favourite toy. Still, he was going to try. He asked Cybil what the toy looked like and where she had last seen it.

Cybil told Malcolm she had had her favourite toy this morning, but when she got home she had lost it. She tried to look for it, but couldn't find it. Malcolm said he would try and find it for her.

Malcolm and Cybil finished their afternoon tea. Malcolm put some of the cakes and sweets into his pockets and set off in search of Cybil's favourite toy.

Malcolm wanted to find Cybil's toy before his bedtime. Malcolm looked along the street; Cybil's toy wasn't there. He looked behind upside-down trees; it wasn't there. He looked around the bushes; and it wasn't there either.

Malcolm didn't know where else to look, so he decided to use magic. He had seen the magician making coins appear from behind children's ears, and he thought maybe he could make Cybil's favourite toy appear from behind her ear.

Malcolm went back to Cybil; he said a secret magic word, before reaching behind Cybil's ear where he found Cybil's favourite toy appearing in his hand.

Cybil was so excited and grateful to Malcolm. She gave him a big hug and an extra big slice of cake to take home with him.

Malcolm walked home, eating the big chunk of cake and feeling great about helping Cybil. This made him smile and think to himself: 'I'm going to be kind and help people more often.'

As the sun set in the pink sky, and the shadows drew long and thin, Malcolm arrived home, *feeling tired and sleepy*, and, with a big yawn, Malcolm went to bed, *falling deeply asleep*.

Timmy and the Secret Door

As you close your eyes, I'm going to tell you a story about a boy called Timmy.

So with *your eyes closed*, you can listen to me reading this story, and while I read this story, you can *begin to feel relaxed*. And as I read, you can *imagine this story* and begin to *drift off to sleep*. As *you drift off asleep* you *can continue this story in a dream*. And my reading will help *you feel sleepy*, it will help *you feel tired* and it will help *you fall asleep*.

Timmy had black scruffy hair and bright blue eyes. He loved carrots and ate carrots with every meal. This made his skin look slightly orange and made him able to see in the dark better than other children.

Timmy lived in an old house where all the walls were covered in wooden panels. One day, while Timmy was in his bedroom playing 'Teddy can fly', Teddy flew into the wall. When Timmy went to get teddy, he noticed that the wooden panel Teddy had bounced off of was loose. Timmy picked up Teddy and took a closer look at the panel.

Timmy noticed that the panel was in fact a secret door. He slowly and carefully opened the door to reveal a secret tunnel. Timmy held onto Teddy's hand, and walked slowly into the tunnel. It was dark in the tunnel. Once Timmy was in the tunnel, he stood still for a moment to let his eyes adjust to the dark. He was glad he had eaten all his carrots.

Once he could see better in the dark, Timmy began walking with Teddy along a path behind the wall. Timmy felt excited as he walked *deeper* into the tunnel. After a few minutes, he discovered some stairs. He decided to walk down the stairs slowly. He could see that there were ten steps, so he walked down, counting how many steps were left as he went.

Ten. Timmy stepped on to the top step. *Nine, eight.* Timmy walked down the stairs slowly. *Seven, six, five.* Timmy could see that he was halfway down the stairs. *Four, three, two.* Timmy wondered what was at the bottom of the stairs. *One.* Timmy stepped off the bottom step and found himself in a secret room.

The secret room had a faint glow to it. The light was coming from a small hole on the far side of the room.

Timmy walked over to the hole and put his eye to it, in order to see what he could see.

As he put his eye to the hole, Timmy noticed it was a secret spyhole which allowed him to see outside the front of his house. He could see what was going on in the street.

Timmy watched. Cars drove past, children played, and adults talked to each other. 'This is exciting!' thought Timmy. He felt like a spy on a secret mission.

Timmy wondered what his secret mission was, and would he be brave enough as a spy to complete his mission?

Timmy looked around and noticed his sister, Mary, outside, playing in a sandpit in the front garden. He wondered whether his mission could be to do with his sister.

Timmy watched Mary playing. He could see that she was playing with a doll and a tea set. It looked like they were having a tea party at the seaside. It couldn't be them he was supposed to spy on. He could see his next-door neighbour, Mrs Oppletop. He wondered if maybe it was her he should be spying on.

Mrs Oppletop was carrying a cage with a sad-looking cat in it, out to her car. 'Maybe she is trying to kidnap that cat, and I need to rescue it?' thought Timmy.

He wondered how he would find out. He could see through the spyhole, but didn't know how he could find out why Mrs Oppletop had the cat in a cage - why had she put the cat in her car? He had to look for clues.

Timmy watched as Mrs Oppletop walked back to her house. Timmy went back to his room to put on his disguise. He wore his dad's baseball cap and his mum's big round sunglasses. He knew he wouldn't be recognised now.

Timmy then went out into the front garden and hid behind the hedge. He had to know why the cat was in the cage and whether it needed rescuing. He looked around, trying to find a way of getting closer to the car.

Mrs Oppletop had left the car door open when she had gone back inside her house. Maybe he could sneak over to the car and take a look.

Timmy started to edge closer. He crept through the hedge slowly, getting *deeper and deeper absorbed* in his role as a spy. He found being a spy exciting.

Just when Timmy was about to reach the car, he saw Mrs Oppletop coming back out of her house. Timmy quickly hid behind a big tree that stood in his front garden. He saw his mum coming out of his house and heading towards Mrs Oppletop.

'Hello Mrs Oppletop,' his mum said. 'Are you off anywhere nice?'

'Just going away for a few days. You know how it is; sometimes you want to *just take some time to relax.*'

'*Take some time to relax*?' Timmy thought to himself. 'Why does Mrs Oppletop want to *take some time to relax*?' All Timmy ever saw Mrs Oppletop doing was lying in her back garden wearing a big floppy hat, covered head to toe in thick white suncream, and dressed in an old-fashioned yellow and pink swimming suit.

Timmy was getting more curious by the minute. He had to listen for more information.

His mum was making a good spy's assistant. She was asking Mrs Oppletop all the questions he couldn't ask without revealing himself. She found out that Mrs Oppletop was heading to the seaside for a few days but had to stop off at someone called Evette's on the way.

Timmy wondered why she was taking a caged cat with her to the seaside. 'Cats don't like water,' Timmy said to himself.

His mum didn't seem to be too bothered; he couldn't understand why. Timmy thought maybe his mum hadn't seen the cat in the cage, so she didn't know Mrs Oppletop was kidnapping the cat. If only he could make his mum aware, then she would do something about it.

As a spy, Timmy felt he had to let his mum know what he had found out.

Timmy's mum had gone back inside the house. The spy quietly and sneakily followed, trying not to be seen by Mrs Oppletop, who was still outside the front of her house.

Once inside, Timmy went over to his mum and told her what he knew about the cat and the kidnapping, and that he had heard her and Mrs Oppletop talking about going away for a few days and seeing Evette first. He explained: he thought that maybe Evette was going to help to kidnap the cat.

Timmy's mum explained that Mrs Oppletop was going on holiday for a few days but her cat Sparkles had been feeling poorly; the vet had asked her to bring him in for a few days to check that he was okay.

Timmy hoped that Sparkles was going to be alright. He was glad that Mrs Oppletop wasn't kidnapping Sparkles, but he did still think it was odd she needed to go on holiday and *relax*.

After a few days, Mrs Oppletop returned home. Timmy saw her arrive and could see that Sparkles was looking much happier. He was rubbing himself against the cage, as if he wanted to be let out. Mrs Oppletop got the cage out of the car and opened it. Sparkles ran out and started to roll around on the grass in the front garden.

Timmy went out to ask Mrs Oppletop if he could play with Sparkles. She let him, and they played from teatime right through to bedtime. Timmy slept well that night, dreaming of more adventures as a spy with Teddy.

The Princess and the Magical Kitten

As you close your eyes I'm going to tell you about a princess called Polly.

So with *your eyes closed*, you can listen to me reading this story, and while I read this story, you can *begin to feel relaxed*. And as I read, you can *imagine this story* and begin to *drift off to sleep*. As *you drift off asleep* you *can continue this story in a dream*. And my reading will help *you feel sleepy*, it will help *you feel tired* and it will help *you fall asleep*.

Polly the princess lived in a beautiful palace surrounded by well-kept gardens, full of colourful flowers, trees and bushes shaped like different animals. There was a bush shaped like a swan, a bush shaped like a fish, and a bush shaped like a bear.

The grass in the garden was green and soft; it was so soft it tickled your feet if you walked around with no shoes on. Polly loved walking in the garden with no shoes on. She would *just relax* and close her eyes and slowly walk around, enjoying the smell of all the flowers.

With her eyes closed, walking around, she would count down each step from ten to one, so that she knew where she was in the garden.

'*Ten, nine, eight,*' Polly said as she walked slowly around the garden. '*Seven, six, five.*' She could feel the tickling of the grass between her toes. '*Four, three, two.*' Polly knew she was nearly by a bush in the garden. '*One.*' On the count of one, Polly knew she had to stop walking and change direction. Polly loved playing this game in the garden.

Polly always dressed in princess dresses, and wore her brown hair in two plaited ponytails. Polly loved being a princess, but sometimes found it lonely and so would play games on her own.

One day, Polly was walking around the garden listening to birds singing in the trees, and feeling the grass tickling her feet. She thought to herself that she would like to have a tea party. She had seen her mummy, the queen, having tea parties - they looked so grown-up.

Polly asked her mummy if she could have her friends round for a tea party.

'No, Polly,' the queen replied. 'You can't have friends around today.'

Polly didn't like this. She crossed her arms and scrunched up her face and sat on the floor sulking.

This didn't do her any good. The queen had said no - and when the queen says no, the answer is no.

It didn't take Polly long before she got bored of sulking. She decided then that she wanted to do something different, something more fun. Sometimes it was boring being a princess. She lived in a beautiful palace, she had beautiful clothes, but she wasn't often allowed friends over to visit, so she would get lonely. She wanted to find something really fun to do.

Polly still wanted to have a tea party, but how was she going to convince her mummy? As she thought to herself, Polly sat down under her favourite tree, closed her eyes and began to think: how could she possibly have a tea party?

While Polly was sitting with her eyes closed and thinking, she started to hear a purring sound.

'Purr, purr, purr.'

At first, Polly thought the purring was just in her mind, so she ignored it and carried on *drifting deeper* into her thoughts. Then she heard it again, closer this time.

'Purr, purr, purr'

Polly immediately knew this time that it wasn't in her mind. She opened her eyes and there, lying on its back on the ground in front of her, was a small black and white kitten. The kitten seemed to enjoy the grass as much as Polly.

Polly stroked the kitten; it purred even more. While she was stroking the kitten, Polly thought to herself, 'I wish I was allowed a tea party with my friends.'

Suddenly her mummy, the queen, came back out into the garden and strode over towards Polly. She sat down next to her, and said, 'If you would like a tea party with your friends, you can have a tea party with your friends.'

Polly jumped up with joy with a big smile on her face. She bounced up and down, exclaiming: 'Really? Really?! Really?!?'

'Yes. Really, Polly,' said her mummy.

Polly thought to herself that she would have to prepare, and she would have to invite all of her friends. Polly picked up the kitten, ran inside the palace and up to her room.

'What should I wear? What should I wear?' Polly said to herself.

She had so many clothes that she didn't know what she should choose. While Polly was deciding, the kitten sat quietly on the bed. Eventually, Polly found a blue sparkling dress to wear.

Next, she had to invite her friends. Being a princess, she had lots of friends - they just weren't normally allowed to visit. She contacted all of them. She knew this afternoon's tea party was going to be the best. She then went and told the cooks what they had to prepare. All she was missing were the decorations to make the tea party look pretty.

Polly stood in the garden, gently stroking the purring black and white kitten, as she looked at the table and chairs that had been laid out for her tea party. 'It looks very boring,' thought Polly, 'I wish it was all sparkly and pretty, with ribbons and fairy lights, and colourful material.'

Just then, lights began to swirl around in a mist as colours filled the air. When the lights, colours and mist cleared, Polly could see a beautiful table ready for her tea party - with ribbons and lights and sparkling stars, and colourful materials.

She wondered whether, somehow, the kitten was magical. When she was under the tree wanting a tea party after her mummy had said no, she was stroking the kitten and her mummy came over and said she could have the tea party. When she wanted the table to be prettier, she was stroking the kitten and the table became pretty. Polly decided to try something. She stroked the kitten while she said she wanted her favourite pop band to come and play.

Her mummy came out into the garden. 'Polly, dear. Just to let you know - we have got a pop band coming to play for your tea party.' Polly was so excited. The kitten was magical! She had heard about magic lamps that you rub, and out pops a genie, but never magical kittens.

During the tea party Polly wanted to show off her new kitten. She kept stroking the kitten and making different wishes. All of her friends were impressed, but the kitten was now getting sad. Polly was acting as though she only liked the kitten because it could make her wishes come true.

After the party, when all of Polly's friends had gone home, Polly went to bed. She took the kitten up to bed with her. When Polly got into bed, the kitten walked away. Polly tried to call the kitten back, but it just looked at her, then turned and continued to walk away. Polly didn't know why the kitten was behaving like this.

She got out of bed and followed the kitten, but every time she caught up with the kitten and tried to pick it up, it walked away faster and struggled to keep moving away. Polly tried to talk to the kitten, but the kitten ignored her.

Polly tried to think what might be wrong with the kitten. 'Have I upset you?' she asked. The kitten turned to face Polly.

Polly spoke with the kitten for a while before realising that the kitten was upset that she was just using the kitten to get what she wanted. She was not being friendly and kind with the kitten, and it thought she didn't want to just spend time with the kitten.

The kitten had become friends with Polly, because it could see that Polly needed a friend. However, once Polly had realised the kitten was magical, she had simply used the kitten rather than being friends back, so the kitten didn't feel this true friendship; it wanted to be friends with someone who would like it for who it was, not what it could do.

Once Polly understood this, she said sorry to the kitten, they became best of friends and she finally went back to bed to *go to sleep*, with the kitten *sleeping peacefully* on its own little bed beside her.

The Magical Unicorn

Close your eyes as I tell you a story about the magical unicorn.

So with *your eyes closed*, you can listen to me reading this story, and while I read this story, you can *begin to feel relaxed*. And as I read, you can *imagine this story* and begin to *drift off to sleep*. As *you drift off asleep* you *can continue this story in a dream*. And my reading will help *you feel sleepy*, it will help *you feel tired* and it will help *you fall asleep*.

Cindy was a short girl with a big heart. She had light hair and dark eyes, and wore a beautiful green dress. Cindy had a magical unicorn called Oracle.

Oracle was pure white with a long, spiral, pointed horn on his head. The horn was glowing white. Oracle was able to fly, and when he flew, it was as if he was galloping on a bridge of sparkling lights.

One day, when Cindy was out riding on Oracle, she heard a faint little sound coming from the edge of the forest.

Cindy decided to investigate, so she guided Oracle down to the ground and headed towards the noise.

As she grew nearer, she noticed that the sound was coming from a tiny baby monkey that had lost its mummy. Cindy went over to the little baby monkey and could see its big sad eyes. She saw that the monkey was scared.

'Don't be scared, little monkey,' Cindy said in a soft, kind and caring voice. 'I'll help you find your mummy.'

Cindy didn't yet know how she was going to help the little baby monkey find its mummy, but she knew she had Oracle - together, they would help. Cindy knew that they would find the baby monkey's mummy.

Cindy picked up the baby monkey and helped it up on to Oracle's back, before climbing onto the saddle herself. Once on Oracle, Cindy decided to *go deeper* into the jungle, in search of the monkey's mummy.

She didn't know where to start looking, but Oracle was a magical unicorn. Oracle was able to see into the past and the future. Cindy whispered into Oracle's ear: 'Can you look back and see the past, and find out where the monkey came from?'

Cindy then had to count down from ten to one and, on the count of one, Oracle would get an image in his mind of when the baby monkey last saw his mummy.

'*Ten*,' Cindy counted. '*Nine, eight, seven, six.*' Cindy hoped that this would work. She held on to the baby monkey in a comfortable and caring embrace. '*Five, four, three, two, one.*'

On the count of one, Oracle got an image in his mind of the baby monkey's mummy, swinging through the trees. The baby monkey was hanging on to his mummy's back when, all of a sudden, he slipped and fell as his mummy bumped into a tree. He landed on the ground, and it looked like his mummy tried to find him. She would probably still be there looking for him.

The baby monkey had also tried to find his mummy, and it looked like they had both gone looking for each other in different directions.

Cindy and Oracle knew where to start looking for the baby monkey's mummy now. They flew over to the bit of the forest where the baby monkey had fallen off. They tried to listen for the sound of the mummy monkey, but they couldn't hear anything. They went *deeper* into the forest, and called out for the baby monkey's mummy. But still, they didn't get any reply.

The baby monkey looked sad and scared. All he wanted was his mummy. Cindy comforted the baby monkey and stroked his head, helping him to *fall asleep comfortably*. She wanted to find his mummy before he woke up.

As Cindy and Oracle kept on searching, following the path that the baby monkey's mummy had taken while looking for her son, Cindy had an idea. Cindy remembered that, when Oracle flies, it is as if he is flying on a bridge of sparkling lights. So she thought: if Oracle could fly in the sky in the pattern of the words 'BABY MONKEY CALL', maybe the mummy monkey would see it and know to call out. That way, they could hear it, then they would know where the mummy monkey was.

Oracle flew up high above the forest and flew in a pattern, making the words BABY MONKEY CALL. They then flew down lower to see if the mummy monkey had seen it and was calling.

There was no call.

They then flew a bit *deeper* into the forest and, flying over this bit of forest, they made the pattern BABY MONKEY CALL in the sky again. Cindy wasn't going to give up hope, the mummy monkey couldn't have gone much further into the forest from where the baby monkey had been dropped. Cindy and Oracle flew even deeper still into the forest, high into the sky, and once more made the pattern BABY MONKEY CALL.

All of a sudden, Cindy could hear the sound of a monkey calling out from below. A beaming smile spread across her face. She knew instantly that this was the mummy monkey. Cindy patted Oracle on the side of the neck, and with that, they flew down towards the sound of the monkey calling.

As they got closer to the top of the forest they could see a monkey jumping around and calling out. Oracle galloped over to the mummy monkey. She instantly saw her baby asleep in Cindy's arms. Cindy could see the happiness in the monkey's eyes at seeing her son, and in seeing that he was alright.

Cindy handed over the baby monkey, and as she did, he woke up. He looked excited to see his mummy, he climbed into her arms and gave her a big hug, before jumping back over on to Oracle and giving Cindy a cuddle too. The mummy monkey also hugged Cindy, and gave her a piece of fruit as a gift.

Cindy and Oracle knew this wasn't going to be the last time they saw these monkeys. They had made some new friends now.

The monkeys swung off in to the trees, and disappeared *deep* into the forest. With this, Cindy gave Oracle a little nudge with her feet - he trotted up into the sky and galloped back towards her home.

Once home, Oracle went into his stables, and settled down for the night, and Cindy went indoors. Cindy told her mum all about her adventures, about how she had found a baby monkey and helped the monkey find its mummy, and about how happy she was to see the monkeys so happy.

Cindy's mum praised Cindy for how kind and caring she had been, and told Cindy it was now her bedtime. Cindy went up to bed, her mum tucked her in and read her a bedtime story. This made Cindy *very sleepy*. Her mum then kissed Cindy gently on the forehead before saying, 'Goodnight Cindy, *sleep* well.'

Cindy then fell *asleep comfortably* and slept all through the night.

The Spaceman and the Dinosaur

Close your eyes as you listen to me reading this story about the spaceman and the dinosaur.

So with *your eyes closed*, you can listen to me reading this story, and while I read this story, you can *begin to feel relaxed*. And as I read, you can *imagine this story* and begin to *drift off to sleep*. As *you drift off asleep* you *can continue this story in a dream*. And my reading will help *you feel sleepy*, it will help *you feel tired* and it will help *you fall asleep*.

One night, Jonny fell asleep. As he drifted *deeper and deeper asleep*, Jonny began to dream about meeting a spaceman. The spaceman landed in his back garden in his spaceship.

Jonny had never been on a spaceship before, so he asked the spaceman whether he could go inside his spaceship. The spaceman, who wore a white spacesuit with a white helmet, said that Jonny could come aboard the spaceship.

Jonny walked up the ramp to the door and inside. He was excited because he was about to find out what the inside of a spaceship looked like. The spaceman walked up the ramp behind Jonny.

The door opened with a hiss and a clang, and Jonny walked into the spaceship, followed closely by the spaceman. Once in the rocket, Jonny started to look around. He wanted to go and explore.

The spaceship was very large. Jonny walked down the first corridor and found some rooms that looked like bedrooms. He then went up to the next level where he found a games room, full of toys and a pool table. Jonny stopped to play for a while, before the spaceman said they needed to go to the bridge, which is where they fly the spaceship from.

Jonny and the spaceman travelled in the lift up to the top of the spaceship, and they entered the bridge.

'Put on your seatbelt,' the spaceman said to Jonny. 'We are going to take off and go on a journey.' Jonny buckled his seatbelt as the spaceman began to get the spaceship ready for take-off.

The spaceman pressed a big red button that started a countdown from ten to one, and on the count of one, the spaceship would start its ascent into space.

'*Ten, nine, eight.*' The countdown was slow, and with each count Jonny grew more excited. '*Seven, six, five.*' Jonny could hear the rumble beginning in the spaceship, as the engines started up, ready for take-off. '*Four, three, two, one.*'

On the count of one, the whole spaceship began to shake and rattle. The rumble from the engines sounded like thunder. Jonny could feel himself being pushed back in his seat as the spaceship rose into the sky.

After about thirty seconds, the rumbling began to *go quiet*. The spaceship stopped shaking and rattling. Jonny began to *relax*, as everything inside the spaceship seemed to come to a standstill.

Jonny felt funny, he didn't know why, but something seemed different.

'You can undo your seatbelt now, Jonny,' said the spaceman.

Jonny undid his seatbelt and went to stand up, but when he tried to stand up, he just floated up out of his seat. Now the spaceship had reached space, Jonny discovered he was weightless.

'Wow!' Jonny said with a big grin. He pushed off of his seat and floated over to the window. He looked out of the window and could see the Earth below him. He could see white clouds, green land and blue sea. The Earth looked like a giant colourful marble against the black background of space.

Jonny looked out of another window, in the other direction, and he could see lots and lots of stars, along with what looked like a giant colourful cloud stretching across his whole view. 'It's beautiful!' Jonny said.

Jonny had never been into space before this point. But now that he had, he definitely wanted to come back here again.

'It's time to go home,' the spaceman said.

Jonny was disappointed, he wanted more time in space - he didn't want to go home yet.

The spaceman turned the spaceship towards the Earth, ready to head home, but while the spaceship was heading home, it passed through a strange purple cloud. The spaceman had never seen a cloud like it. When the spaceship came out of the other side of the cloud, the Earth below looked different.

The spaceman had to continue his journey down to Earth, although he didn't know what was going on. Nor could he understand why the Earth looked so different.

'Put your seatbelt back on, Jonny,' said the spaceman. 'We are about to enter the Earth's atmosphere.'

Jonny got back in his seat and put his seatbelt on.

As the spaceship entered the Earth's atmosphere, it began to shake and rattle like it had done when they took off. The spaceship travelled *deeper and deeper* into the Earth's atmosphere, getting closer and closer to the ground.

After a minute or so, the shaking and rattling stopped and the *rest* of the flight down to the ground was *calmer and more comfortable.*

When the spaceship landed, Jonny and the spaceman went outside to see where they were.

Thud, thud, thud, thud.

It looked like they were near a forest of giant trees.

Thud, thud, thud, thud.

Jonny and the spaceman could hear the footsteps of what sounded like a giant, walking along. Then they heard a sound a bit like a whale's call.

Jonny and the spaceman looked around, but they couldn't see where the sound was coming from. They walked around the other side of the spaceship and still couldn't see its source.

Then, all of a sudden, one of the trees seemed to lift itself up out of the ground. Jonny realised it wasn't a tree, but rather it was the leg and foot of a giant dinosaur. The leg swung forward, before thudding back down onto the ground, followed by three more legs doing the same.

Jonny looked up to the top of the trees, where he noticed a small head on top of a long neck, eating the leaves among the treetops.

Jonny and the spaceman wanted to investigate further. They ran over to the giant dinosaur. They didn't know how they'd got here, or even where 'here' was. Maybe passing through that strange purple cloud was like passing through a wormhole that made them travel back in time millions of years, right back to when dinosaurs were on Earth.

Jonny and the spaceman climbed up into one of the tall trees to get a closer look. The dinosaur swung its head towards them to eat leaves from the tree they were in. Jonny broke off some leaves and fed these to the dinosaur. He thought to himself, 'This is the most exciting night of my life,' as the dinosaur ate the leaves and almost seemed to smile at Jonny for being so kind.

After a while, the spaceman told Jonny it was time to go. The spaceman was going to try to fly back through the purple cloud and see if it might take them back to their own time.

Jonny and the spaceman climbed down from the tree, went back to the spaceship and prepared for take-off. Jonny wasn't going to forget tonight. He had fed a dinosaur, met a spaceman and flown in a spaceship in space!

The spaceship took off with a rumble and headed back into space. The spaceman steered his way towards the purple cloud. When they came out of the other side and looked down at the Earth, they saw that it all looked normal again. The spaceman was relieved.

'Let's get you home,' the spaceman said to Jonny as he flew the spaceship down to Earth.

The spaceman landed the spaceship back in Jonny's garden. Jonny climbed down and said goodbye to the spaceman before making his way indoors and up to bed.

Jonny slept well that night, dreaming vividly of spaceships and dinosaurs.

The Swift and the Swallow

Close your eyes as I tell you a story about the swift and the swallow.

So with *your eyes closed*, you can listen to me reading this story, and while I read this story, you can *begin to feel relaxed*. And as I read, you can *imagine this story* and begin to *drift off to sleep*. As *you drift off asleep* you *can continue this story in a dream*. And my reading will help *you feel sleepy*, it will help *you feel tired* and it will help *you fall asleep*.

Taylor Swift and Lucy Swallow were best of friends. Every year, they would meet up at the same house and talk about what they had been doing and where they had been over the past twelve months.

Taylor's nest was just above the bedroom window of a young girl called Suzy. Suzy used to love hearing the sound of the swift arriving. Taylor's husband used to arrive shortly after her. Suzy lived in a house on a farm. Lucy's nest meanwhile was in the barn, out the back of the house.

This year, when Taylor and Lucy arrived at their nests, something didn't seem right. The young girl Suzy appeared to be sad. Taylor and Lucy used to see a lot of Suzy; she was often playing in the garden as they flew around high up in the sky.

But this year, Suzy was just sat in her room. She wasn't smiling or playing outside, and she didn't seem to be excited by the arrival of Taylor and Lucy.

Taylor wondered what was wrong with Suzy, and whether there was anything she could do to help. Taylor couldn't land and hop around very well, though, so she asked Lucy if she could talk with Suzy.

Lucy flew to Suzy's bedroom window and sat on the window ledge peering in. She tapped lightly with her beak on the glass. 'Suzy, Suzy,' Lucy said. 'Suzy, are you okay? Can we help you?'

Suzy stayed sat on her bed, still looking sad. Lucy tried tapping on the window again.

Tap, tap, tap.

'Suzy, are you okay?'

Suzy thought she heard a noise and a soft squeaky voice. She looked up and around, but couldn't see anybody there. Then, she heard the tapping at the window again, so she decided to investigate.

She walked over to the window and saw a tiny little swallow perched on the ledge. 'Suzy, are you alright? I'm Lucy,' the swallow squeaked.

Suzy explained to Lucy that she was playing in the garden the other day when a magpie flew down and stole a necklace that her mum had bought for her as a birthday present, and she hadn't been able to get it back.

Lucy said that she and Taylor - the swift who nests in her rafters above her bedroom window - would see if they could find the necklace and get it back for her.

Suzy smiled graciously and said, 'Thank you,' before then heading to bed. She hoped beyond all hope that Lucy and Taylor would find her necklace for her. Knowing that the birds were going to help, Suzy fell *asleep*, feeling hopeful that she may indeed get her necklace back.

While Suzy was *drifting deeper and deeper asleep*, Lucy went back to Taylor and told her all about the magpie and

Suzy's necklace. They had to decide where to start looking and how they were going to find the lost necklace.

Taylor had an idea where the magpie might be, as she had seen a few magpies in a nearby field. Taylor was fit and fast-moving, so she could fly up high and find the magpies, but she couldn't hop around on the ground very well. Lucy wasn't so fast, but she could hop around on the ground and investigate while Taylor kept watch.

Taylor flew over the field. She could see the magpies on the ground. It looked like they were a gang. Taylor flew back and told Lucy where the magpies were.

The two birds went to confront the magpies. Taylor couldn't land, so she just circled overhead while Lucy flew down to talk to the magpies.

'Have you seen a little girl's necklace?' asked Lucy

'What if we have, what if we haven't?' one of the magpies replied.

'The little girl would like her necklace back.'

'That isn't going to happen. What we take, we keep'

The magpies weren't going to return the necklace, so Lucy and Taylor were going to have to find out where the necklace was, and then take it back from the magpies themselves.

For the next few hours, Lucy and Taylor flew high up in the sky, circling around and watching the magpies closely. They were trying to work out where the thieves were keeping all their stolen items.

After a few hours they realised that the magpies kept on going into an old rabbit hole. Taylor wondered whether the magpies were keeping their loot down the rabbit hole.

Lucy flew down to take a closer look. She perched in a nearby tree and waited for the magpies to go into the rabbit hole.

It was starting to get dark, but Lucy could just about make out the magpies as they arrived at the hole and walked in. She saw that the birds were carrying jewellery and other small items.

Lucy flew off to tell Taylor what she had seen. They were definitely stealing things and hiding them in the old rabbit hole.

Taylor and Lucy thought of a plan as to how they were going to retrieve the necklace. They also wanted to try to get the magpies to return everything they had stolen to the people from whom they had taken.

Lucy and Taylor flew around the field above the rabbit hole. 'You fly down and hop slowly and carefully up to the hole. Once you are there, I will create a distraction and you can head into the rabbit hole to get the necklace,' said Taylor.

Lucy carefully flew down to the ground without being seen. She then hopped up to the hole, keeping herself hidden from the view of the magpies. Taylor then started flying down at the gang. She was making a lot of noise as she dived at one magpie after another.

The magpies were distracted by this. 'Get her!' one of them cried.

The magpies ran along and took off into the air to try to catch Taylor. While they were chasing Taylor, Lucy crept into the rabbit hole. It was dark, but she could just about see.

Lucy walked deeper and deeper into the rabbit hole looking for items the magpies had stolen. At the end of one long tunnel, Lucy discovered a room full of stolen items. She knew the necklace must be among these items somewhere. She started to search through them all, looking for the necklace.

Taylor continued to evade the magpies. They may have been bigger, but their flying skills were no match for Taylor's moves. Taylor darted down through them, flew up again; dodged left, dodged right. The magpies didn't stand a chance - they were becoming exhausted.

Taylor slowed down a little to try to give them a chance to catch her. She didn't want them to *become so tired* that they would head back to the rabbit hole and ignore her. She had to see Lucy come out of the hole first, before she could let them head back there.

Lucy finally found the necklace and made her way with it back out of the rabbit hole. As she exited the hole, she could see Taylor, still flying around and out-manoeuvring the magpies. She sneaked carefully away from the hole before flying off to take the necklace back to Suzy.

Once Taylor saw Lucy fly away, she began to accelerate and to exhaust the magpies. Eventually, the magpies were *so tired* they decided to land. Taylor couldn't fly down and land with them, so she just circled above them and addressed them from a distance.

Taylor explained that the magpies were upsetting lots of people by taking their stuff, and asked them how they would feel if someone was stealing from them. The magpies thought about what Taylor was saying, and told her that they would return everything they had stolen in the morning.

Taylor flew home and spoke with Lucy. Lucy explained that she had successfully returned the necklace to Suzy.

The next morning Suzy woke up to see her necklace on the window ledge outside the window. She opened the window, grabbed her necklace and put it on, before then thanking Taylor and Lucy for their help.

The magpies got up early and returned everything they had taken to their rightful owners. They felt a sense of pleasure from seeing others smile as they were reunited with lost items. The magpies felt that maybe it would feel better to help others, than to take from others. So they decided this was what they would do from now on.

Taylor and Lucy got to enjoy the sunny weather; they took great pleasure from watching Suzy playing happily in the garden as they flew gracefully in the sky above.

The Caterpillar's Dream

Close your eyes as I tell you a story about the caterpillar's dream.

So with *your eyes closed*, you can listen to me reading this story, and while I read this story, you can *begin to feel relaxed*. And as I read, you can *imagine this story* and begin to *drift off to sleep*. As *you drift off asleep* you *can continue this story in a dream*. And my reading will help *you feel sleepy*, it will help *you feel tired* and it will help *you fall asleep*.

Once upon a time, there was a caterpillar that lived on a leaf. He didn't know how he ended up on the leaf; he just woke up one day, and there he was.

This caterpillar found that he was very lonely on the leaf. Off in the distance, he could see other caterpillars on their own leaves, and all he wished for was to be able to go and play with them.

Robin, the caterpillar, wished that he had wings. He watched other animals fly from flower to flower, from leaf to leaf, and yet he was stuck here on this leaf - all alone.

While Robin dreamed of being able to fly, he munched on the leaf, eating and eating. He thought to himself, 'At least I have this whole leaf to myself to eat. I don't have to share it.'

But deep down, he still wished that he could share his food with a friend.

Robin watched the sun rise, and the sky turn a beautiful shade of blue. He watched the sun setting and the sky changing to orange. And still, all he did was eat.

After the sun had set, Robin drifted *comfortably asleep,* hoping that when he woke up, he would have wings and be able to fly and make friends.

Robin drifted off to *sleep*, and as he drifted *deeper and deeper asleep,* he began to dream of a world where caterpillars had wings to get around - in this world, he could visit any leaf he wanted.

When Robin woke up the next morning, nothing had changed. He was still the same caterpillar. He was still on the same leaf, and he still just felt like eating and eating.

Robin spent the day, munching on the thick green leaf, while he gazed off over the countryside, dreaming about being able to fly.

Just then, a beautiful butterfly landed on the flower next to the leaf Robin was eating. 'Why so sad?' asked the butterfly.

'I wish I could fly. I am stuck here on this leaf, and it is lonely. I would like to meet other caterpillars and go exploring,' the caterpillar replied.

'You will be able to fly one day,' said the butterfly.

'How can you be so sure?'

'Trust me.'

The butterfly flew off and went to another plant. Robin wondered how the butterfly could be so sure that he would, one day, be able to fly.

That night, like the previous night Robin, fell *asleep, dreaming* of being able to fly. As he drifted *deeper and deeper asleep,* so his dreams became more real to him. He loved *drifting off to sleep* and enjoying his dreamworld. In his dreams, Robin could be and do anything he wanted.

The next morning, Robin again woke up, still wishing he could fly. He felt it was boring, spending each day just eating. Today, though, something felt a bit different. Robin felt a bit unusual.

He spent the first part of the day eating, but then, as the sun was beginning to set, he felt like he wanted to be wrapped up and hugged. He started making a small jumper for himself, then attached it to the bottom of the leaf so that he wouldn't fall out when he put it on.

He then carefully made the jumper around him, first knitting the jumper around the bottom part of his body, and gradually attaching it right up to his head.

Robin didn't know why he felt the need to sleep in a jumper this night; he just had a feeling and had to act on it. Robin made the jumper up over his head, until it was like he had made his own little tent.

Robin felt calm and peaceful inside this jumper. So calm and peaceful, in fact, that he fell asleep more comfortably than he had even done before.

While Robin slept he dreamt of flying. He drifted deeper and deeper asleep, and didn't realise that he didn't wake up the next morning. Robin didn't wake up the morning after that either, or the morning after that. In fact, Robin slept for about two weeks.

When Robin woke up, he felt strange. He felt like he had been asleep for ages. Robin started to nudge his head out from inside the jumper. Something about him felt different, but he didn't know what.

As he pushed out of his jumper with his head, he noticed he had antennae on his head. He thought to himself that this was unusual - where had they come from? They weren't there when he had gone to sleep. He kept pushing out from the jumper, and noticed his back, too, felt different.

When he pushed out of the jumper a bit more he realised that his back felt different because there were what looked like extra bits of skin there.

After what seemed a very long time struggling to get out of the jumper, Robin managed to break his legs out. It shouldn't have been a struggle to get his legs out, because Robin had short and stumpy legs. But as he finally escaped, he noticed that he no longer had short and stumpy legs; now, they were long and elegant.

Robin tried to move around a bit, but found it awkward. Something didn't feel right. Then, he noticed that when he breathed in a certain way, the bits of skin on his back seemed to blow up, almost like a balloon.

Robin focused on blowing up the bits of skin. As he did, he noticed they were getting larger and larger, until they became beautiful, colourful wings. Robin was amazed. His dreams had come true: he had become a butterfly.

Robin carefully tested out flapping his wings. He flapped enough to lift himself off the leaf. He was able to fly. He felt hungry and went to take a bite of the leaf, but all that happened was that a new long tongue came out and sucked at the leaf.

He thought to himself, 'What am I supposed to do for food?'

Then he remembered the butterfly that visited the plant. That butterfly was drinking something from inside the flowers. Maybe that was what he was supposed to do now.

Robin flew over to a flower. It took him a few tries to get used to flying, and to land where he wanted. But after some practice, he mastered it.

On the flower, Robin carefully aimed his tongue down into the plant and tried to drink up with his tongue. It felt weird, but the juice was so sweet and tasty. Nothing like the bitter leaf he had been eating.

After drinking some of the juice from the plant, Robin noticed that there were lots of butterflies everywhere. What's more, now he could go and see any of them!

He jumped off the plant and flew over to another butterfly. That butterfly was just as excited as he was. It seemed that many of the caterpillars had become butterflies at the same time!

Robin finally made friends, got to go exploring *and* to have fun. This was his dream come true!

The Boy Who Ran Off to the Circus

Close your eyes as I tell you a story about the boy who ran off to the circus. And with *your eyes closed*, you can listen to me reading this story, and while I read this story, you can *begin to feel relaxed*. And as I read, you can *imagine this story* and begin to *drift off to sleep*. As *you drift off asleep* you *can continue this story in a dream*. And my reading will help *you feel sleepy*, it will help *you feel tired* and it will help *you fall asleep*.

James was a little boy with a cheeky streak. One night, when his parents went to bed James crept out of bed, and sneaked out of the house.

James knew this was a naughty thing to do, but he had heard that the circus was in town. James loved the circus and wanted to join in. He had always dreamt of becoming a circus performer.

To get of the house, James had to creep from his room and down the stairs in the dark. He didn't want to disturb anyone, so he couldn't turn the lights on.

James had remembered how many steps there were to get downstairs. He remembered that there were ten steps; three steps leading down to a landing, and then he had to turn to the left before walking down the final seven steps.

James walked slowly and carefully to the top of the stairs. There was a faint glow into the upstairs landing, from a streetlight outside, so he could just about see where he was going. Once James made it to the stairs he held onto the bannister and began to walk down the stairs slowly. He counted deliberately as he went.

'Ten, nine.' James counted as he took small, slow steps. *'Eight.'* James knew he was now on the landing and had to turn to the left to continue down the stairs. *'Seven, six, five,'* James continued, slowly and quietly. *'Four, three, two, one,'* he whispered to himself. James had safely made it to the bottom of the stairs.

He was now stood at the front door. James opened the door and walked nervously out into the street. He was scared and excited all at the same time. He had seen a map, and so knew the way to the circus. They were only set to be in town for a few days. So, if he was going to join them, he would have to do it now, for he didn't know when they might come back.

As James walked along the dark streets, trying to keep under the street lights, he thought about his parents. He thought about whether they would be upset when they found that he wasn't home. Still, he hoped that they would be happy for him, because he really wanted to join the circus.

James had left a letter for his parents so that they would know where he was and what he was doing. He didn't want them to worry.

After what seemed like a long walk, James could see the top of the circus tent at the end of the road. He smiled and began to walk faster towards the tent. James was only ten, but he hoped the circus would let him work for them and would teach him how to become a performer.

When James arrived at the circus, he found that it was all locked up, and everyone was asleep. This wasn't a surprise to James. After all, it was only 4am. But he had hoped that someone would be awake to let him in.

Because everyone was *asleep*, James had to wait outside the circus until the performers woke up. James thought the circus opened at 9am, so the circus performers must have been up by 7am at least, in order to get ready to work and set everything up. James sat down, feeling cold and tired, by the entrance to the circus. He waited.

While he waited, he found himself *drifting off to sleep* from time to time. It seemed like ages until the sun started to rise in the sky, and at that point, he could see circus people coming out of their caravans starting to set up the circus.

Whenever any of the circus people came near the gate, James called to them trying to get their attention. He wanted to let them know that he was going to join the circus. But none of them let him in - or even came over to talk to him.

At 9am, someone came over to the gate and opened it. James tried saying that he wanted to join the circus and asked if he could come in.

'No, lad. If you want to come in, you have to pay like everyone else,' said one of the circus staff.

James explained that he didn't want to come in as a customer, he wanted to come in to join them and be a performer. He explained that he had left home to join the circus. He told them how good he was on the trampoline.

Back at home, meanwhile, James' parents woke up, and when James didn't come down for breakfast despite them calling him, and making him his favourite (egg in an egg cup with dippy soldiers), they went upstairs to his room to check he was okay.

When they saw James was missing, they panicked and got upset. They saw the letter and quickly got dressed to head to the circus to find him.

Back at the circus, James was still trying to convince them to let him in. Then, one of the staff thought maybe he would be safer with them while they called his parents to come and pick him up.

'Come in lad,' said one of the circus staff. 'What's your name?'

'James.'

'Well, James. Why don't you come in for a moment while we call your parents?'

James went with the circus staff. They walked him to the big tent. James thought this was so exciting. He was finally in the big tent, maybe they would let him join. James told the circus staff they didn't need to call his parents because he had left them a note to say he has gone to join the circus.

They explained to James that his parents would certainly be worried about him, even if he had left them a note. So, because of this, they needed to call his parents.

James gave them his parents' telephone number, but by the time they were being called, James' mum and dad had already arrived at the circus looking for their son.

While the circus staff went to fetch James' parents, one of the performers stayed with James and said he would teach him some of the circus performers' techniques.

James was excited by this. He was helped onto a wire to walk across. This wasn't as easy as he thought it would be. He kept falling off. Luckily, the wire was only a metre or so off the ground and there were safety mats, so James didn't get hurt.

After talking with circus staff, James' parents came running into the big tent. They ran up to James, grabbing him and giving him a big hug. They told James how much he had scared them and how dangerous it was to run away like that.

James apologised and said he didn't think it would have upset them because he had left them a note. But, he explained, now that he was here and had been trying to do some of the circus tricks, he didn't think he was ready to join the circus after all.

One of the circus performers came over to James and said that he could attend a circus skills course to learn some of the tricks and stunts that circus performers do. James was excited about this.

'Joining the circus isn't for someone as young as you,' the performer said. 'But if you come back when you are a grown-up, and you have learnt the skills and still want to join, then we may let you.'

James smiled and thanked the performer, before leaving the tent and heading home with his parents to have his breakfast.

Adventure of a Time-Travelling Worm

Close your eyes as I tell you a story about an adventure of a time-travelling worm.

So with *your eyes closed*, you can listen to me reading this story, and while I read this story, you can *begin to feel relaxed*. And as I read, you can *imagine this story* and begin to *drift off to sleep*. As *you drift off asleep* you *can continue this story in a dream*. And my reading will help *you feel sleepy*, it will help *you feel tired* and it will help *you fall asleep*.

Sid was an interesting worm. He wasn't like other worms; wormholes he made led to other points in time, not just in space.

One day, when it was raining outside, Sid was keeping warm and dry in a wormhole. He could hear the pitter-patter of rain falling on the soil above, but he remained *comfortable* in his hole.

Sid found the sound of rain *relaxing*. He enjoyed lying in his wormhole with his eyes closed, listening to the sound of the rain which made him *drift deeper and deeper in to a relaxed dreamy state.*

Sid didn't like going out into the rain, because he was only little - raindrops seemed really big to him. If a raindrop hit him, it would hurt.

As a worm, Sid also didn't like it when it was too hot and sunny, because he would get too dry and sunburnt. He liked a nice grey day, just after the rain, when the soil would be moist and easy to dig through, and the air fresh and clean.

Once the rain stopped, Sid decided to go outside and see what the weather was like.

As he poked his head out of the hole, he saw that it was clear and dry, and the ground was still nice and damp. Sid slithered out of his wormhole and around the ground. He wondered what he was going to do today.

Every time Sid burrowed into the ground he created a wormhole, and when he burrowed out of the ground again, the wormhole he created could lead anywhere... He never knew where he would come out.

Sid sometimes enjoyed creating time-travelling wormholes. Other times, he wished he could be like other normal worms.

Sid burrowed into the ground, and the *deeper* he went the darker it got. He continued burrowing *deeper and deeper*, then after digging deep into the ground, Sid turned upwards again and began to dig up to the surface. It was always a scary and exciting experience, not knowing what he would discover when he reached the surface.

As Sid approached the surface he could hear the sound of hundreds of fast-moving footsteps. It sounded like a stampede. When Sid poked his head out of his wormhole, he saw hundreds of horses galloping around with cowboys on them. It looked like Sid had appeared in the Wild West.

Sid didn't like the Wild West. It was too dry. He wanted to get out of here. Just as he went to turn and head back to where he had come from, he saw a big black bird trying to grab a worm from the ground. The other worm was trying to hide from the bird, but it wasn't going to be able to hide for long.

Sid knew that he had to do something, but he didn't know what. He didn't have control over his time-travelling abilities, so he couldn't dig his way over to the other worm to save them. If only it were that easy!

Sid tried to carefully slide over to the other worm without being noticed by the bird. As he got closer and closer, he could see that the bird was noticing movement. The bird hadn't yet noticed it was a worm moving, but it was clearly aware that something was moving.

Suddenly, the bird started coming for Sid. Sid quickly burrowed into the ground. As he burrowed up to the surface again he didn't know where he was going to be. He knew he could go back out the way he had just come in, but the bird might be there waiting for him.

He burrowed up to the surface, and as he approached the surface, he listened closely to try to find out where he was. He couldn't hear any noise. As he poked his head out of the wormhole and looked around, he saw men in ninja suits creeping around.

Sid thought to himself, 'I wish I had the skills of a ninja, then I could save that other worm.'

Sid watched as the ninja silently moved past and disappeared into the shadows. Sid began burrowing again. He dug down *deeper and deeper* into the soil, just where he had done before. If he could find out how to control his time-travelling ability, then he could easily save the other worm. He wondered if digging *deeper* or shallower could change where he travelled in time.

When Sid dug back up to the surface, this time he found himself in a futuristic world. Cars didn't have wheels, they hovered off the ground. They also drove themselves. There were tall towers, as tall as the sky, stretching up into the clouds. And there were lots of plants and animals.

Sid had travelled 200 years into the future. In this time, robots did most of the work, it seemed, and people got to spend all of their time having fun and playing. The people loved spending time out in nature.

Sid liked this world, but he couldn't stay here. He had to burrow again.

Sid burrowed down again, digging *deeper and deeper*, before tunnelling back up to the surface. This time, he came out in the middle of a carnival. There was coloured string and confetti everywhere. This gave Sid an idea. He decided to get some of the coloured string and take it back with him to the Wild West.

Sid went back down the hole he had just come out of (where he popped out in the future). He then went over to the other hole he'd come out of, where he had seen the ninjas. He then went down that hole and, carefully, he popped his head up in the Wild West. He pushed the coloured string out in front of him.

As he was pushing the string out, the bird's beak grabbed it. The bird was clearly distracted by the string, trying to work out what it was.

While the bird was distracted, Sid quickly slid over to the other worm to rescue it. He wrapped his tail around the other worm and pulled it to safety under a cart.

'Oh, thank you, thank you,' the other worm said. 'I'm Felicity. Thank you for saving me!'

Sid told Felicity that they would have to get away from the bird before he became bored of the string and came looking for them.

Sid dug down into the soil, closely followed by Felicity. He didn't know how she would react when they exited the wormhole and she discovered that they were no longer in the Wild West.

Sid didn't spend much time with other worms; he didn't really have any friends. But Felicity seemed to quite like him. He hoped she wouldn't be scared and put off him because he was different.

Sid began digging up towards the surface again. As he poked his head out of the surface, he saw that he was in a beautiful garden full of colourful plants, and plenty of soft soil to dig through.

Felicity popped her head out of the hole and was confused and amazed, wondering where they were and what had happened. Sid explained about being a time-travelling worm that could dig wormholes.

Felicity didn't seem bothered by this at all, she still wanted to be with Sid. She said they could stay living in this beautiful garden together. Sid said he didn't think that was possible because he never knew where his wormholes would go.

Felicity told him, though, that she could make all the wormholes for them to live in, and he could make wormholes to different places. And they would always have this garden to come back to.

Sid was happy with this, and the two of them lived in the garden happily ever after.

The Puppy Who Wanted to Play

Close your eyes as I tell you a story about the puppy who wanted to play.

So with *your eyes closed*, you can listen to me reading this story, and while I read this story, you can *begin to feel relaxed*. And as I read, you can *imagine this story* and begin to *drift off to sleep*. As *you drift off asleep* you *can continue this story in a dream*. And my reading will help *you feel sleepy*, it will help *you feel tired* and it will help *you fall asleep*.

Patches was a small black puppy with white markings, who just wanted to play. He woke up this morning already playful.

'Play with me, play with me!' Patches said excitedly as he ran into his owner's bedroom.

Liz, Patches owner, was still trying to *sleep*. 'Let me *sleep*,' she said to Patches.

But Patches didn't want to let Liz *sleep*. He wanted to play. Liz pulled the duvet cover over her head. 'Go away Patches, I'm *sleeping*.'

Patches left Liz's room and went to see Alli, Liz's daughter.

'Play with me, play with me,' Patches said to Alli, jumping up and down on her bed.

'No, Patches, let me *sleep*.' Alli said.

Patches was sad. 'Why does no-one want to play with me?' He went downstairs. He really badly wanted to find someone to play with.

He went over to Tiddles the cat. 'Tiddles, will you play with me?'

Tiddles was *resting, sleeping* on a small and comfy cat bed by the radiator. 'No, Patches, I *want to sleep*, find someone else to play with.'

Patches still couldn't find anyone to play with him.

He thought, maybe he could ask Gary the parrot, so he did. 'Gary, will you play with me?'

Gary agreed to play one round of hide-and-seek.

'You go and hide, I'll count from ten down to one, and then I will try to find you.' Gary said.

Patches got excited - finally! Someone to play with him! Patches ran off to hide as Gary started counting.

'*Ten, nine, eight,*' Gary counted.

'Where to hide? Where to hide?' Patches asked himself as he ran around the living room trying to find somewhere to hide.

'*Seven, six, five.*'

Patches could hear Gary counting down, he knew he didn't have much time. He tried hiding behind the curtains, but his feet poked out the bottom. He tried hiding behind a plant pot, but he was too big. He tried hiding under a chair, but he could easily be seen there.

'*Four, three, two.*'

Patches knew that Gary had nearly finished counting, so he had to quickly choose somewhere to hide.

'*One*. Ready or not, I'm coming.'

Patches had found a place to hide, just in time.

Gary began searching for Patches. Being a parrot, he thought he could fly around the room and have a bird's eye view, and maybe that way he would spot Patches.

'Are you behind the curtain?' Gary said, as he checked behind the curtain.

Patches wasn't there.

'Are you under the table?' Gary said, as he checked under the table.

Patches wasn't there.

Gary flew around the room wondering where to look next.

'Are you behind the plant pot?' Gary said, as he checked behind the plant pot.

Patches wasn't there either.

Gary didn't know where to look next. 'Where could Patches be hiding?' Gary said to himself.

Patches tried not to laugh as he heard Gary searching for him.

'Are you behind the door?' Gary said, as he checked behind the door.

Still no Patches.

Gary thought he had looked everywhere in the living room. He really didn't know where else to check.

Patches thought to himself, what a good hiding place he had found, to be able to stay hidden from Gary for so long. He had wanted someone to play with, and now he was playing. Patches was having such fun.

After checking many other places and not finding Patches, Gary checked inside the footstool. There was Patches!

'Found you Patches!' Gary said. 'Now I'm going back to *rest*. I'm *tired and sleepy*.'

Patches was having so much fun, he didn't want to *rest*. He just wanted to play.

'Gary, please keep playing with me!' Patches begged.

But Gary said no, he wanted to *go to sleep now.*

Patches had to go and find someone else to play with. He thought to himself, who else could he ask?

Patches went back to Tiddles the cat. 'Will you play with me now?'

Tiddles just shrugged and curled up into a ball. 'No, I'm still *sleeping.*'

Patches went and asked Liz. 'Will you play with me now?'

Liz just tucked herself up even tighter in bed. 'No, I'm still *sleeping.*'

'Why does everyone *just want to sleep* all the time?' thought Patches as he went in to see Alli. 'Maybe she will be awake now.'

Patches opened Alli's bedroom door. 'Will you play with me now?' he asked.

'No, I'm trying to *sleep*. Why don't you find fun things to do by yourself for a while?'

'Like what?' said Patches curiously.

'Have you thought of painting? Or drawing a picture, or using the sticks in the garden and making jumps to see how high you can jump over, or making a running track in the garden and seeing how fast you can run around the track, or building a den in the garden?'

Patches hadn't thought about any of these ideas. He was really excited by them. They all sounded so much fun… He couldn't wait to try all of these ideas out.

Patches went out into the garden, he started by getting some paints and painting a picture of his paws. This turned out to be very messy. Patches had to use old newspapers to make his paws clean, so that he didn't make a mess back in the house.

He then made a running track in the garden. He timed himself running around the track to see how fast he was. Then he ran around the track over and over again, trying to run faster than he had run before.

Patches did this for a while, but eventually it got very exhausting, he was *beginning to feel sleepy and tired.*

Patches decided that, because he was *feeling sleepy,* he should build a den in the garden to *sleep* in.

Patches gathered up lots of wood from the garden and went inside the house to get some old sheets from one of Liz's cupboard. He then went out to the end of the garden to build his den.

His den had a wooden frame, made from sticks that were in the garden, leaning against a tree. They were then tied to the tree at the top, a bit like a tepee tent. Patches had then put blue sheets around the outside, with a space left at the front to walk in and out of the den.

He put a picnic sheet on the ground inside the tent and got all of the cushions from the living room and put these on top of the sheet.

Patches' den was nice and *comfortable* and cool. He sat there, noticing how the sun was rising higher in the sky, and how it was getting hot in the garden while he stayed cool in his den.

When Alli came downstairs and outside to see what Patches had been doing, she was really impressed with his den. She asked if she could play with him in his den.

Patches said she could, but that he wanted to snuggle up in his den and *have a little sleep first*. He was *tired* from all the hard work. He told Alli he would play with her when he woke up. Then, he closed his eyes, gave a big yawn, and fell *fast asleep*.

The Magical Journey Asleep

(Unlike the other stories in this book, this story is more advanced and targeted and full of the various techniques to help your child to sleep)

Close your eyes as I tell you a story about Milton's magical journey *asleep*.

So with *your eyes closed*, you can listen to me reading this story, and while I read this story, you can *begin to feel relaxed*. And as I read, you can *imagine this story* and begin to *drift off to sleep*. As *you drift off asleep* you *can continue this story in a dream*. And my reading will help *you feel sleepy*, it will help *you feel tired* and it will help *you fall asleep*.

Every night just before bed Milton would get excited. He loved to *fall asleep*. He looked forward to bedtime even when he wasn't *tired and sleepy*, because bedtime was when he could *drift off to sleep* into a magical land of fun and make believe where he could do anything he wanted.

This magical land of fun and make believe was a land of dreams. The land of dreams could only be accessed by going to bed, *getting sleepy*, snuggling up into your covers and *drifting off to sleep*.

As bedtime drew near Milton got ready for bed, and would *start to yawn*, he then went and brushed his teeth, and climbed into bed *ready to sleep*. One of his parents would then take some time to read him as story, as he lay in bed starting to *drift off to sleep*.

As Milton started to *drift off to sleep*, he would *start to dream about the story* he was being read, and would *begin to go on a magical journey* into his land of dreams.

One day when Milton was *drifting off to sleep* listening to his mum reading a bedtime story to him he could feel himself travelling to his land of dreams.

It felt like he was flying through a magical tunnel flying *deeper and deeper* down the tunnel towards that land of dreams.

The tunnel was dark with flashes of purple light and colour. The tunnel seemed to sparkle with what looked like millions of twinkling stars all around him.

Milton was excited as he continued travelling through this tunnel. He knew this flying, floating feeling meant he was *falling asleep* and getting closer to his land of dreams.

Off in the distance Milton could see the exit of the tunnel. It looked like a green meadow with trees. He never knew where he would be when he arrived in his dreamland, he was always excited to find out.

As Milton continued to fly through the purple shimmering tunnel towards his dreamland, he could feel himself *drifting off to sleep*.

Once Milton felt himself *drifting off to sleep* he liked to notice how his body was *falling asleep* as his mind travelled off to his land of dreams.

Milton thought about his head 'what does it feel like?' he said to himself.

He noticed he could feel his hair, he could feel the pillow under his head, he could feel his eyes being closed, and the breathing through his nose.

As Milton let himself *relax more*, he noticed that the muscles in his head and around his face were *beginning to relax*. It was like his face and head was *falling asleep*.

Milton wondered 'how will my body *continue to relax* next?'

As Milton thought this, he noticed the *relaxing* had moved down from his head and into his shoulders. He could feel his shoulders beginning to *fall asleep comfortably*. And this *relax*ation, this *falling asleep comfortably* feeling that was spreading carefully moved down into his arms.

He liked to *pay close attention to that relaxation*, to see which arm was becoming most *relax*ed fastest. He didn't know if the *relax*ation would get to his left hand or his right hand first.

Once both arms and hands were *relax*ed the *relax*ation, the *falling asleep comfortably* feeling began to spread down through his body.

Milton loved this *falling asleep* feeling, because to *really enjoy dreamland* his body needed to *be fast asleep*, so that his mind could *enjoy being in the dreamland*.

Milton noticed that both his arms now felt heavy, and at times he noticed it was like they had *fallen asleep* so *deeply* and so *comfortably* that he almost couldn't feel them.

As Milton's body began to *relax*, he could see that he was getting nearer to the end of the purple sparkling tunnel. He could see his *dreamland getting closer and closer*.

The *falling asleep feeling spread comfortably* down through Milton's body and into his legs. Like with his arms, Milton wondered which leg the *falling asleep* feeling will spread down fastest. He wondered which foot will *fall asleep* first.

Milton knew once his body had totally *fallen asleep* from the top of his head to the tips of his toes he would *arrive in dreamland*.

As the *falling asleep* feeling finally reached Milton's toes he noticed how *sleepy and comfortable* his body felt as his drifted away from being aware of his body, to *drifting into dreamland*.

In dreamland now, Milton looked around. He found himself stood up on a bank at the top of a long green garden. Around the outside of the garden was tall trees full of rustling leaves. At the end of the garden was a play park with swings, and climbing frames, and roundabouts, and lots of other fun rides.

Milton walked slowly down the ten steps from where he was standing, down to the main part of the garden below. As he walked down the steps, he slowly counted down to himself how many steps were left.

'*Ten*,' Milton said quietly to himself before stepping onto the first step. '*Nine, eight, seven*,' Milton could feel himself *become deeper absorbed in the dreamland* as he walked down the steps. '*Six, five, four*,' Milton could see he only had a few steps left before stepping on to the soft, cool, green grass. '*Three, two, one.*'

Milton stepped gently onto the cool green grass. As he took a deep breath he could smell the beautiful smell of all the flowers in the garden.

Milton walked down to the play area to spend some time playing before he went on his latest adventure.

After playing for a while Milton went to an old wooden door at the back of the garden. He could feel the warmth of the sun on his face, and see dancing rays of sunlight shining through the trees.

He opened the magical old wooden door wondering what adventures would be there for him today. And as he opens the door you can *dream about Milton's adventures* with him while *you sleep* and *have pleasant dreams all night long.*